My

D0744980

in
Basketball

A Sports Record Book

WARNER ⦿ TREASURES™
Published by Warner Books
A Time Warner Company

Warner Treasures is a trademark of Warner Books, Inc.

Warner Books, Inc.
1271 Avenue of the Americas
New York, NY 10020

 A Time Warner Company

Book design by Leandra Jones
Cover design by Lisa C. McGarry

My Year in Basketball is produced by becker&mayer!, Ltd.

Printed in Singapore.
First Printing: March 1996
10 9 8 7 6 5 4 3 2 1

ISBN: 0-446-91135-6

My Year in Basketball

A Sports Record Book

by _____

My Year in Basketball

What better way to keep track of your progress through the upcoming season than by keeping a diary of your team's successes!

All you have to do is carefully observe every game you play in—and after the game is over, take a few moments to fill in the blanks on the pages for that game. Do this after every game and, by the time the season wraps up, you'll have a permanent diary of your year in basketball.

It's easy, fun to do, and best of all, by writing a complete record of your sports season you're writing your own book! And when the season comes to an end, you'll be able to place your diary in a treasured spot on your bookshelf.

Be sure to write your name on the title page of your sports journal. After all, how many kids your age can claim to have written a book?

MY YEAR IN BASKETBALL

Year: _____

My name: _____

My team's name: _____

My coach's name: _____

My uniform number: _____

My team's league: _____

My height: _____

My weight: _____

MY TEAMMATES

_____

_____

_____

_____

_____

_____

_____

_____

_____

GAME 1

Date of game: _____

Our opponent: _____

Final score: _____

Positions I played: _____

Assists: _____

Field goals attempted/made: _____

Free throws attempted/made: _____

Total points: _____

Total rebounds: _____

Steals: _____

Fouls: _____

Turnovers: _____

Plays I made well: _____

_____

Things I need to work on: _____

_____

**What the coach told me
about my performance:** _____

_____

_____

Dribble with Both Hands

The first thing to learn in basketball is how to dribble the ball. The second thing to learn is how to dribble the ball with both hands.

Don't worry about shooting the ball through the hoop, just get used to the feel of the ball. Make a conscious effort to dribble the ball first with one hand, and then with the other.

By developing a feel for the ball you'll be able to dribble it without even looking at it. Try closing your eyes when you practice dribbling.

When it comes to dribbling, it makes no difference how tall—or short—you are. Magic Johnson, one of the great ball handlers of all time, is 6 feet 9 inches tall. Muggsy Bogues, perhaps the best point guard in the NBA, is only 5 feet 3 inches tall.

GAME 1

MY SEASON SO FAR

Team Record _____

Positions Played _____

Field Goals Attempted/Made _____

Free Throws Attempted/Made _____

Assists _____

Steals _____

Turnovers _____

Fouls _____

How I Would Rate My Play So Far:
(SCORE 1–10: 1-OUTSTANDING; 5-AVERAGE; 10-POOR)

Passing _____

Shooting _____

Defense _____

Rebounding _____

Team Player _____

Practicing Your Shot

For any basketball player who's younger than the age of eleven, hoisting a ball up into the air and into a basket takes a tremendous amount of energy and strength. Around the age of eleven or twelve kids find that their arm strength has developed enough so that they can actually begin to work on their shot.

The only way to improve your shooting skills is to go out on a court and practice, practice, practice. Shoot by yourself, with friends, or in a game. But just keep on shooting.

That's the only way you're going to improve.

Have NBA shooters gotten better over the years? In 1961–1962, Walt Bellamy led the league in field goal percentages with a .519 average. In 1993–1994, Shaquille O'Neal led the NBA with a .599 average.

GAME

Date of game: _____

Our opponent: _____

Final score: _____

Positions I played: _____

Assists: _____

Field goals attempted/made: _____

Free throws attempted/made: _____

Total points: _____

Total rebounds: _____

Steals: _____

Fouls: _____

Turnovers: _____

Plays I made well: _____

_____

Things I need to work on: _____

_____

**What the coach told me
about my performance:** _____

_____

_____

Passing the Ball

There are several basic passing styles in basketball, and you should be well trained in all of them.

The most basic style is the chest pass, in which you hold the ball with both hands in front of your chest and pass the ball directly to a teammate. Be sure to handle the ball with your fingertips—you can direct the pass better.

The bounce pass is used when you want to make a pass that won't be swatted away by an opponent. It's particularly effective when trying to get the ball to a teammate who's being closely guarded.

The looping or lob pass is made to taller teammates who are closer to the basket than you are. Use it when you want to get the ball over an opposing player's head.

You're credited with an assist whenever you throw a pass to a teammate who then scores a basket. John Stockton, the all-time NBA leader in assists, usually averages about thirteen assists per game.

MY SEASON SO FAR

Team Record _____

Positions Played _____

Field Goals Attempted/Made _____

Free Throws Attempted/Made _____

Assists _____

Steals _____

Turnovers _____

Fouls _____

How I Would Rate My Play So Far:
(SCORE 1–10: 1-OUTSTANDING; 5-AVERAGE; 10-POOR)

Passing _____

Shooting _____

Defense _____

Rebounding _____

Team Player _____

Playing Defense

Every coach will tell you that the very best teams in basketball play excellent defense. That's because even though you can't always control how well you're going to play offensively in a game, you can always control how well you play defensively.

Playing defense requires nothing more than making it difficult for your opponent to score. That means you've got to stay close to him or her, between your opponent and the basket, and always be ready to recover a rebound while keeping your opponent away from the ball.

You'll be surprised how valuable you'll become to your team when you play solid, consistent defense.

Stealing the ball from your opponent takes quickness, skill, and daring. The best defensive players in the NBA average about two or three steals per game.

GAME

Date of game: _____

Our opponent: _____

Final score: _____

Positions I played: _____

Assists: _____

Field goals attempted/made: _____

Free throws attempted/made: _____

Total points: _____

Total rebounds: _____

Steals: _____

Fouls: _____

Turnovers: _____

Plays I made well: _____

_____

Things I need to work on: _____

_____

**What the coach told me
about my performance:** _____

_____

_____

Advanced Dribbling

There was a time, not too long ago, when dribbling a ball between one's legs was never done. Nobody knew how to do it. As players got better and began to experiment with their dribbling skills, they found it was easier to change direction by dribbling the ball through their legs.

Like most skills, this takes practice. First, spread your legs out with one foot in front of the other. Make certain there's plenty of room between your legs. Dribble the ball with one hand and bounce it through your legs to your other hand. Do this simple drill as many times as you can.

Most kids find that they have to look down at the ball when they dribble. Practice so you can look straight ahead on the court when you dribble the ball.

MY SEASON SO FAR

Team Record _____

Positions Played _____

Field Goals Attempted/Made _____

Free Throws Attempted/Made _____

Assists _____

Steals _____

Turnovers _____

Fouls _____

How I Would Rate My Play So Far:
(SCORE 1–10: 1-OUTSTANDING; 5-AVERAGE; 10-POOR)

Passing _____

Shooting _____

Defense _____

Rebounding _____

Team Player _____

What's the Best Sneaker?

Turn on the television these days and all you see is advertising for different brands of basketball shoes. Some come in brilliant colors, others have air pumps, and all are endorsed by the biggest names in basketball.

The simple fact of the matter is that it really makes no difference which basketball shoe you wear. None of them make you jump any higher, run any faster, or play better defense.

What you want is a shoe that fits correctly, protects your ankles (high-top sneakers are best), and can be easily laced and tied.

Up until fifteen years ago, basketball sneakers were fairly standard in style and fashion. Most of the players in the NBA and on college teams wore simple high-top, white canvas sneakers.

Date of game: _____

Our opponent: _____

Final score: _____

Positions I played: _____

Assists: _____

Field goals attempted/made: _____

Free throws attempted/made: _____

Total points: _____

Total rebounds: _____

Steals: _____

Fouls: _____

Turnovers: _____

Plays I made well: _____

_____

Things I need to work on: _____

_____

**What the coach told me
about my performance:** _____

_____

_____

Protective Goggles

You'll note that more and more players in the NBA are wearing protective goggles. Most players wear them to protect against getting an opponent's elbow or finger stuck in their eye—an accident that can occur when going up for a rebound in traffic.

Although the goggles might feel a bit goofy at first, after a while they become comfortable, and you'll learn to like wearing them! If you wear them both in games and in practice, before long they'll become an essential part of your game gear.

Most players who normally wear eyeglasses off the court find that wearing soft contact lenses is the most comfortable way to see better when playing in a game. Other players may opt for prescriptive goggles that also provide protection on the court.

MY SEASON SO FAR

Team Record _____

Positions Played _____

Field Goals Attempted/Made _____

Free Throws Attempted/Made _____

Assists _____

Steals _____

Turnovers _____

Fouls _____

How I Would Rate My Play So Far:
(SCORE 1–10: 1-OUTSTANDING; 5-AVERAGE; 10-POOR)

Passing _____

Shooting _____

Defense _____

Rebounding _____

Team Player _____

What About a Mouth Guard?

Just like protective goggles, many of today's players have started to wear mouth guards when they play ball. They're relatively inexpensive (less than $2), and they can be a real help in protecting your teeth—especially if you wear braces!

Like goggles, it may take a little time to get accustomed to wearing the mouth guard. Some new players find that it's difficult to talk, or even yell, with a guard. You will adjust very nicely to the mouth guard as you get more and more used to wearing it.

Try one. Your parents—and your dentist—will be very happy!

Mouth guards come in a variety of colors, from white to yellow, to red to black. If you want to wear a mouth guard, think about what color you'd like!

Date of game: _____

Our opponent: _____

Final score: _____

Positions I played: _____

Assists: _____

Field goals attempted/made: _____

Free throws attempted/made: _____

Total points: _____

Total rebounds: _____

Steals: _____

Fouls: _____

Turnovers: _____

Plays I made well: _____

_____

Things I need to work on: _____

_____

**What the coach told me
about my performance:** _____

_____

_____

Snap Quiz

Who holds the career record for scoring 50 points or more in a game?

If you guessed Michael Jordan, that's only good enough for a second place finish. When Michael rejoined the Chicago Bulls in 1995 after his year of professional baseball, he had a career total of 26 games in which he scored more than 50 points.

But as good as Michael is at scoring, he's still got a long way to go to catch Wilt "The Stilt" Chamberlain. The 7-foot Hall of Fame center scored more than 50 points in a game a whopping 118 times in his long and successful career.

The irony about Wilt Chamberlain is that even though he was a terrific scorer from the field, he was never a very consistent free throw shooter. His lifetime average at the foul line was only 51 percent.

MY SEASON SO FAR

Team Record _____

Positions Played _____

Field Goals Attempted/Made _____

Free Throws Attempted/Made _____

Assists _____

Steals _____

Turnovers _____

Fouls _____

How I Would Rate My Play So Far:
(SCORE 1–10: 1-OUTSTANDING; 5-AVERAGE; 10-POOR)

Passing _____

Shooting _____

Defense _____

Rebounding _____

Team Player _____

Shooting Foul Shots

Most kids practice shooting foul shots in a calm, leisurely fashion—perhaps after practice or by themselves when they get a chance.

That's okay for fun, but remember this: When you shoot a foul shot in a game, chances are you're sweaty, you're breathing hard, and there are people watching you. And if you're shooting for needed points, you're also going to be nervous.

There's a big difference between shooting foul shots in your backyard and shooting them during a game. When you go to the foul line, try to develop your own routine. The more you stick to it, the more consistent you'll be at the foul line.

The leader in free throw percentages in the NBA is Mark Price, with a lifetime average of just over 90 percent at the foul line.

Date of game: _____

Our opponent: _____

Final score: _____

Positions I played: _____

Assists: _____

Field goals attempted/made: _____

Free throws attempted/made: _____

Total points: _____

Total rebounds: _____

Steals: _____

Fouls: _____

Turnovers: _____

Plays I made well: _____

_____

Things I need to work on: _____

_____

**What the coach told me
about my performance:** _____

_____

_____

Basic Defenses

The two most common defenses in basketball are the "man-to-man" and the "zone" defenses.

With man-to-man you match up with a specific opposing player and guard her or him througout the whole game. If you get separated from your man and have to defend another player, make certain to yell out, "Switch!" so another teammate can guard your man.

With a zone defense, your defensive responsibility is to guard an area of the court—the zone—not a player.

Sometimes, a coach will alternate between man-to-man and zone throughout the game. When the game starts, be sure you know what kind of defense you're playing.

In high school and college ball you can play either man-to-man (woman-to-woman) or zone defenses. In the NBA zone defense is against the rules.

MY SEASON SO FAR

Team Record _____

Positions Played _____

Field Goals Attempted/Made _____

Free Throws Attempted/Made _____

Assists _____

Steals _____

Turnovers _____

Fouls _____

How I Would Rate My Play So Far:
(SCORE 1–10: 1-OUTSTANDING; 5-AVERAGE; 10-POOR)

Passing _____

Shooting _____

Defense _____

Rebounding _____

Team Player _____

Boxing Out an Opponent

Any coach will tell you that out-rebounding your opponent is the key to success in a basketball game. The best way to ensure your chances of getting a rebound is by "boxing out" your opponent.

That doesn't mean you're supposed to wrestle with your opponent. If the player you're guarding takes a shot, you should turn toward the basket and get ready to grab the rebound. Keep your arms high in the air, and be ready if the ball bounces directly to you. Guard your opponent by positioning your backside so that he or she can't race around you and get the rebound for themselves.

The best NBA rebounders of all time are Kareem-Abdul Jabbar, Wilt "The Stilt" Chaimberlain, and Bill Russell.

GAME 7

Date of game: _____

Our opponent: _____

Final score: _____

Positions I played: _____

Assists: _____

Field goals attempted/made: _____

Free throws attempted/made: _____

Total points: _____

Total rebounds: _____

Steals: _____

Fouls: _____

Turnovers: _____

Plays I made well: _____

_____

Things I need to work on: _____

_____

What the coach told me about my performance: _____

_____

_____

What about "Ball Hogs"?

At some point in your basketball career you're going to encounter a ball hog. That's a player who insists that he or she handle the ball most of the game, either dribbling up the court, or taking all the shots.

Ball hogs think the team can't win unless they're the star.

Nobody likes a ball hog. Share the ball, pass it around, and remember that you're on a team for a reason: teamwork. If there's someone on your team who hogs the ball all the time, let the coach know. You can't solve a problem if you don't talk about it with the coach. After all, that's what coaches are for!

The 1972–1973 NBA Champion New York Knicks were considered by many fans to be one of the greatest teams of all time. Why? Because all the players were gifted passers and unselfish in handling the ball.

MY SEASON SO FAR

Team Record _____

Positions Played _____

Field Goals Attempted/Made _____

Free Throws Attempted/Made _____

Assists _____

Steals _____

Turnovers _____

Fouls _____

How I Would Rate My Play So Far:
(SCORE 1–10: 1-OUTSTANDING; 5-AVERAGE; 10-POOR)

Passing _____

Shooting _____

Defense _____

Rebounding _____

Team Player _____

Proper Shooting Technique

When you shoot, it's sometimes difficult to get the right grip on the ball if your hands are small.

To remedy this, cradle the ball on your fingertips—not in the palms of your hands. Let your fingers and wrists do the work. Bring the ball back above your head, and fling the ball off your fingertips toward the basket. As you follow through, your shooting wrist should flick the ball.

Also, be certain to get enough arc, or height, on your shot. Line drives don't give the ball much chance to bounce around the rim and fall in. If you get enough arc on your shot, you'll be surprised how many of your shots will hit.

The rim should be exactly 10 feet high when measured from the bottom of the iron rim to the floor below.

Date of game: _____

Our opponent: _____

Final score: _____

Positions I played: _____

Assists: _____

Field goals attempted/made: _____

Free throws attempted/made: _____

Total points: _____

Total rebounds: _____

Steals: _____

Fouls: _____

Turnovers: _____

Plays I made well: _____

_____

Things I need to work on: _____

_____

**What the coach told me
about my performance:** _____

_____

_____

Do Tall Kids Have an Advantage?

Yes and no. When it comes to rebounding, being taller definitely helps. But being tall can be a disadvantage for some kids when it comes to dribbling. Successful shooting really depends on the individual player.

For example, NBA star Muggsy Bogues is only 5 feet 3 inches tall. Scottie Pippen was only 6 feet tall in high school, but grew another eight inches when he was in college!

As you can see, it doesn't matter whether you're tall or short; it's just how well you play the game!

Consider this: Charles Barkley is only 6 feet 5 inches tall and Dennis Rodman is 6 feet 8 inches tall. Neither one of them is the tallest on his team, yet both are great rebounders.

MY SEASON SO FAR

Team Record _____

Positions Played _____

Field Goals Attempted/Made _____

Free Throws Attempted/Made _____

Assists _____

Steals _____

Turnovers _____

Fouls _____

How I Would Rate My Play So Far:
(SCORE 1–10: 1-OUTSTANDING; 5-AVERAGE; 10-POOR)

Passing _____

Shooting _____

Defense _____

Rebounding _____

Team Player _____

Develop Your Wrists!

Wrist strength is very important in basketball. Just like baseball, where a batter needs strong wrists to swing a bat, or hockey, where a player needs strong wrists to handle a stick, basketball players need strong wrists to handle the ball.

After all, the stronger your hands are, the more control you'll have when dribbling and shooting. To develop more strength, try squeezing a tennis ball whenever you get a spare moment. When your wrists get stronger, so will your game!

Did you know that Danny Ainge used to play in the major leagues with the Toronto Blue Jays? Or that former Knick great Dave DeBusschere used to pitch for the Chicago White Sox? You probably thought Michael Jordan was the first to play professional basketball and baseball!

Date of game: _____

Our opponent: _____

Final score: _____

Positions I played: _____

Assists: _____

Field goals attempted/made: _____

Free throws attempted/made: _____

Total points: _____

Total rebounds: _____

Steals: _____

Fouls: _____

Turnovers: _____

Plays I made well: _____

_____

Things I need to work on: _____

_____

**What the coach told me
about my performance:** _____

_____

_____

Shooting Bank Shots

The backboard, or glass, can be your friend when it comes to scoring. On those shots when you're shooting from an angle at the basket, sometimes the best approach is to aim at a mark on the backboard. With practice, your shot will bounce off that spot and into the hoop.

Like all shots, shooting a bank shot takes time and practice, and every sharpshooter will tell you that it's easier to shoot at a mark on the backboard rather than the entire hoop. If you develop a soft touch, the bank shot has a much better chance of going in the hoop because of the higher arc you have to put on the ball.

Shoot the ball with inner confidence. If you start worrying that your shots won't go in, then you've missed even before you've released the ball.

MY SEASON SO FAR

Team Record _____

Positions Played _____

Field Goals Attempted/Made _____

Free Throws Attempted/Made _____

Assists _____

Steals _____

Turnovers _____

Fouls _____

How I Would Rate My Play So Far:
(SCORE 1–10: 1-OUTSTANDING; 5-AVERAGE; 10-POOR)

Passing _____

Shooting _____

Defense _____

Rebounding _____

Team Player _____

What if You Don't Make the Cut?

As with all sports, there are no guarantees in basketball. The sports pages are full of great athletes who have had to overcome all sorts of obstacles to become top players.

For example, there was once a young basketball player in North Carolina who hoped that one day he'd see his dreams come true on the court. But as a sophomore, he was cut from his high school varsity team.

Fortunately Michael Jordan didn't give up and worked even harder on his game. The following year he made the varsity. You must know the rest of the story.

Always remember this: You miss 100 percent of the shots you don't take!

GAME

Date of game: _____

Our opponent: _____

Final score: _____

Positions I played: _____

Assists: _____

Field goals attempted/made: _____

Free throws attempted/made: _____

Total points: _____

Total rebounds: _____

Steals: _____

Fouls: _____

Turnovers: _____

Plays I made well: _____

_____

Things I need to work on: _____

_____

What the coach told me about my performance: _____

_____

_____

Speaking of Frustration...

Even the best in the game— the pros in the NBA—have to cope with tough shooting nights. You'd be amazed at how many great players have had nights in which nothing—zip—goes into the hoop.

Take the nightmare game that Tim Hardaway of the Golden State Warriors played on December 27, 1991. Try as Tim might, he just couldn't find the range. By the time the final horn sounded, Hardaway had attempted 17 baskets—and hadn't made a single one!

Keep that statistic in mind the next time you have a rough night on the court.

On the other side of the ledger: Who holds the record for most consecutive shots made? No surprise—Wilt Chamberlain once made 18 shots in a row in a 1967 game.

GAME 10

MY SEASON SO FAR

Team Record _____

Positions Played _____

Field Goals Attempted/Made _____

Free Throws Attempted/Made _____

Assists _____

Steals _____

Turnovers _____

Fouls _____

How I Would Rate My Play So Far:
(SCORE 1-10: 1-OUTSTANDING; 5-AVERAGE; 10-POOR)

Passing _____

Shooting _____

Defense _____

Rebounding _____

Team Player _____

The Out-of-Bounds Line

If you are handling the basketball and any part of your foot touches any part of the out-of-bounds line, the referee will blow the whistle, stop play, and hand the ball over to the other team.

In basketball, you have to be constantly aware of the side and end lines. This can get particularly tricky when you're under the basket trying to go up for a rebound or lay-up. It's easy to lose track of where the lines are when your eyes are focused on the basket.

A personal foul is committed when a player interferes with an opposing player's movements. A technical foul is called when a player displays unsportsmanlike behavior, either on the court or on the sidelines.

11 GAME

Date of game: _____

Our opponent: _____

Final score: _____

Positions I played: _____

Assists: _____

Field goals attempted/made: _____

Free throws attempted/made: _____

Total points: _____

Total rebounds: _____

Steals: _____

Fouls: _____

Turnovers: _____

Plays I made well: _____

_____

Things I need to work on: _____

_____

**What the coach told me
about my performance:** _____

_____

_____

Dealing with Nerves

All basketball players get nervous before a game. It's actually a good thing to be nervous. Why? Because when your heart is pounding and you feel that rush of adrenaline before a game, your body is ready and eager for action. You're at your sharpest. From a mental and physical point of view, you're ready to go.

So, the next time you start getting nervous before a game, don't worry about it—your body is just telling you that it's ready for action!

Legend has it that Bill Russell, the great Hall of Fame center for the Boston Celtics, used to get so nervous that he would throw-up before every NBA game he played. And he played in more than 1,000 games!

MY SEASON SO FAR

Team Record _____

Positions Played _____

Field Goals Attempted/Made _____

Free Throws Attempted/Made _____

Assists _____

Steals _____

Turnovers _____

Fouls _____

How I Would Rate My Play So Far:
(SCORE 1–10: 1-OUTSTANDING; 5-AVERAGE; 10-POOR)

Passing _____

Shooting _____

Defense _____

Rebounding _____

Team Player _____

Finding a Screen

One of the first offensive strategies you should develop is the ability to shoot from behind a "screen." A screen develops when one of your teammates stands a couple of feet in front of you so you can get a clean, unobstructed shot at the basket.

The best screen is usually put up by a good-sized teammate who will be able to block your opponent from waving his or her hands in your face.

If you're on defense and you find yourself up against a screen, try to get around that screen as quickly as possible to guard your opponent. Your job as a defensive player is to keep him or her from taking a shot.

When it comes to accurate shooting, you always want to get a "good look" at the basket. That means you have a few seconds to set yourself straight and take the time to shoot the ball with a good follow-through.

Date of game: _____

Our opponent: _____

Final score: _____

Positions I played: _____

Assists: _____

Field goals attempted/made: _____

Free throws attempted/made: _____

Total points: _____

Total rebounds: _____

Steals: _____

Fouls: _____

Turnovers: _____

Plays I made well: _____

_____

Things I need to work on: _____

_____

**What the coach told me
about my performance:** _____

_____

_____

The Pick-and-Roll

One of the classic basketball plays is the "pick-and-roll."

Here's how it works: As you're dribbling the ball, one of your teammates comes over and plants their body—sets a pick—on one side of the player who's guarding you. You then dribble—or roll— past the pick. Your opponent has to quickly make a decision—try to stay with you by getting around the pick? Or call out "Switch!" to a teammate, so they can swap the players they are guarding?

All this takes place very quick- ly. In the confusion, the team- mate who set the pick can then break for the basket. If the de- fenders are still confused, you should be able to throw your teammate a pass to make a quick score.

Many high school and college basketball coaches design their teams' offensive plays to incorporate the pick-and-roll. Look for it the next time you're watching a basketball game.

12

GAME

MY SEASON SO FAR

Team Record _____

Positions Played _____

Field Goals Attempted/Made _____

Free Throws Attempted/Made _____

Assists _____

Steals _____

Turnovers _____

Fouls _____

How I Would Rate My Play So Far:
(SCORE 1–10: 1-OUTSTANDING; 5-AVERAGE; 10-POOR)

Passing _____

Shooting _____

Defense _____

Rebounding _____

Team Player _____

The Three-Second Rule

Although it's rarely enforced on the playground during pickup games, the three-second rule is always recognized in an organized game.

An offensive player cannot spend more than three consecutive seconds in the "paint." The paint is the rectangular area directly in front of the basket that goes from the baseline out to the foul line.

The three-second rule keeps the players moving in and out of the shooting area. If the referee blows the whistle and charges you with a three-second violation, play is stopped and the ball goes to the other team.

A three-second violation counts as a turnover. There are several other kinds of turnovers, including traveling with the ball, double-dribbling, kicking the ball, stepping out of bounds, and losing the ball to an opponent's steal. Good teams try not to make many turnovers.

Date of game: _____

Our opponent: _____

Final score: _____

Positions I played: _____

Assists: _____

Field goals attempted/made: _____

Free throws attempted/made: _____

Total points: _____

Total rebounds: _____

Steals: _____

Fouls: _____

Turnovers: _____

Plays I made well: _____

_____

Things I need to work on: _____

_____

**What the coach told me
about my performance:** _____

_____

_____

Jumping

Coaches will tell you that the best way to improve your jumping ability is by strengthening your thigh and calf muscles through regular practice.

Wearing leg or ankle weights when you play pickup games is a good way to gain strength. When you start to play without the weights, you'll feel like you can fly! Jumping rope is also an excellent way to strengthen your foot arch and leg muscles. It may sound simple, but jumping rope is a fun way to get stronger.

Many of the NBA's best leapers can not only jam the ball through the hoop, but they can even go an extra foot or more above the rim! Watch them at the league's annual slam-dunk contest during the NBA's All-Star weekend.

GAME 13

MY SEASON SO FAR

Team Record _____

Positions Played _____

Field Goals Attempted/Made _____

Free Throws Attempted/Made _____

Assists _____

Steals _____

Turnovers _____

Fouls _____

How I Would Rate My Play So Far:
(SCORE 1–10: 1-OUTSTANDING; 5-AVERAGE; 10-POOR)

Passing _____

Shooting _____

Defense _____

Rebounding _____

Team Player _____

Hoops on the Playground

It's a lot harder to play basketball on a playground than it is inside a nice, cozy gym. Since a playground is outside, you are always at the mercy of the weather. If it's windy when you're playing, your outside shots are going to be affected by the breeze. If it's a sunny day, you may find yourself squinting to make a shot if the sun is in your eyes.

Playing on asphalt can also be difficult. Cement surfaces can be full of bumps and might also be slippery.

The good news? Just think how much easier it will be to play a game inside when you don't have all of those external distractions!

The famed parquet floor at the Boston Garden (the old home of the Boston Celtics) was full of bumps that drove opposing teams crazy when they dribbled the ball. It was rumored that only the Celtics knew where the bumpy areas were on the floor.

GAME 14

Date of game: _____

Our opponent: _____

Final score: _____

Positions I played: _____

Assists: _____

Field goals attempted/made: _____

Free throws attempted/made: _____

Total points: _____

Total rebounds: _____

Steals: _____

Fouls: _____

Turnovers: _____

Plays I made well: _____

_____

Things I need to work on: _____

_____

**What the coach told me
about my performance:** _____

_____

_____

Develop a Parallel Dream

For millions of kids, going on to play in the NBA is what it's all about. The problem is, the odds of making it to the NBA are pretty slim.

It's essential that you develop a "parallel dream" in life to combat the odds. That is, make certain you have other things you enjoy doing besides playing hoops, in case your NBA dream doesn't come true. Perhaps your parallel dream of becoming a teacher or doctor or lawyer or whatever will come true.

And that's what it's all about.

Senator Bill Bradley of New Jersey used to be a star forward for the New York Knicks. Dave Bing, former star for the Detroit Pistons, now runs his own steel company. And Phil Jackson of the New York Knicks was ready to go to law school before he began coaching the Chicago Bulls.

MY SEASON SO FAR

Team Record _____

Positions Played _____

Field Goals Attempted/Made _____

Free Throws Attempted/Made _____

Assists _____

Steals _____

Turnovers _____

Fouls _____

How I Would Rate My Play So Far:
(SCORE 1–10: 1-OUTSTANDING; 5-AVERAGE; 10-POOR)

Passing _____

Shooting _____

Defense _____

Rebounding _____

Team Player _____

Who Invented the Game?

You might have heard that basketball is truly an American invention, dreamt up by Dr. James Naismith at Springfield College back in the late 1890s. Dr. Naismith needed something that would entertain his physical education students during the cold, wintry months in Massachusetts. Because he used old fruit baskets that were nailed to the wall some 10 feet off the floor, Dr. Naismith had to climb a ladder to retrieve the ball each time a player scored a basket.

In the early years of basketball most players used two-handed set shots. It was only in the 1940s–1950s that players started to develop the one-handed jump shot that is so often used today.

After a little while, somebody thought it could save a lot of time if they merely cut out the bottom of the fruit baskets so that the ball would just go through. Dr. Naismith did just that, and presto—basketball was invented!

GAME 15

Date of game: _____

Our opponent: _____

Final score: _____

Positions I played: _____

Assists: _____

Field goals attempted/made: _____

Free throws attempted/made: _____

Total points: _____

Total rebounds: _____

Steals: _____

Fouls: _____

Turnovers: _____

Plays I made well: _____

_____

Things I need to work on: _____

_____

**What the coach told me
about my performance:** _____

_____

_____

The Best Team of All-Time

There's always debate about the best team in pro basketball. You can make a case for the Chicago Bulls who had three championship seasons, the great Boston Celtic teams of the 1960s, or even the Los Angeles Lakers and New York Knicks.

In terms of the best overall record, that honor goes to the famed Harlem Globetrotters, who have been around since 1929 and have literally won thousands of games and lost only a handful.

What's the secret to the Trotters' success? Well, for one thing, they have great players. But perhaps the most important key to their success is the fact that the Globetrotters are really a touring exhibition team!

What's the best record ever compiled by an NBA team for a season? The 1971–1972 Los Angeles Lakers finished at 69–13. The team with the worst record? The Philadelphia 76ers with 9–73 in 1972–1973.

MY SEASON SO FAR

Team Record _____

Positions Played _____

Field Goals Attempted/Made _____

Free Throws Attempted/Made _____

Assists _____

Steals _____

Turnovers _____

Fouls _____

How I Would Rate My Play So Far:
(SCORE 1–10: 1-OUTSTANDING; 5-AVERAGE; 10-POOR)

Passing _____

Shooting _____

Defense _____

Rebounding _____

Team Player _____

Snap Quiz:
Know the Rules!

Okay, so you think you know the rules of the game, right? If you can, try to answer this easy question:

What is the diameter of the standard NBA rim?

A. 18 inches
B. 20 inches
C. 24 inches

Chances are you've been playing the game for a few years, and you've had a good look at the rim. Give up?

The answer is A: 18 inches.

How many fouls can you commit before you're ejected from a game? In high school and college, committing five fouls sends you off to the showers. In the NBA, it's six fouls before you're out.

GAME 16

Date of game: _____

Our opponent: _____

Final score: _____

Positions I played: _____

Assists: _____

Field goals attempted/made: _____

Free throws attempted/made: _____

Total points: _____

Total rebounds: _____

Steals: _____

Fouls: _____

Turnovers: _____

Plays I made well: _____

_____

Things I need to work on: _____

_____

**What the coach told me
about my performance:** _____

_____

_____

Getting a Step
Past Your Opponent

The thing about playing basketball is that you don't have to be fast—but you do have to be quick. There's a difference.

"Fast" usually refers to an athlete who can run like the wind up and down the court. Being "quick" refers to the first step you take with the basketball. There are a lot of players who are fast, but who aren't necessarily quick with that first move. Likewise, there are lots of players who are quick but not fast.

In basketball, a lot of offensive plays are based on that first move, so being quick is especially important to your game. If you practice moving quickly, your game will improve.

Does being quick help in basketball? Think about Kenny Anderson, Mark Price, or Anfernee Hardaway. Their combination of quickness and athletic ability make them great players and perennial NBA all-stars.

MY SEASON SO FAR

Team Record _____

Positions Played _____

Field Goals Attempted/Made _____

Free Throws Attempted/Made _____

Assists _____

Steals _____

Turnovers _____

Fouls _____

How I Would Rate My Play So Far:
(SCORE 1–10: 1-OUTSTANDING; 5-AVERAGE; 10-POOR)

Passing _____

Shooting _____

Defense _____

Rebounding _____

Team Player _____

How Many Socks Should You Wear?

That may sound like a weird question, but if you have ever developed blisters on your feet from playing basketball, then you know the importance of socks.

You may find it surprising to learn that many players like to wear not one, but two pairs of socks at a time. The first pair is a relatively thin, white athletic sock. Once that's on, a thicker, heavier, white athletic sock goes over the first layer.

One pair of socks prevents your feet from rubbing against the inside of the sneakers, and two pairs of socks provide a little extra padding so there's less chance that a serious blister will occur.

Above all, remember this: It's just a game.

Notes

_____

_____

_____

_____

_____

_____

_____

_____

_____

_____